1866-1991

125th

ANNIVERSARY

HEART AND
PERIMETER

ALSO BY LINDA BIERDS

Flights of the Harvest-Mare (1985)
The Stillness, the Dancing (1988)

HEART AND PERIMETER

POEMS BY

LINDA BIERDS

HENRY HOLT AND COMPANY

NEW YORK

Published by Henry Holt and Company, Inc.,
115 West 18th Street, New York, New York 10011.
Published in Canada by Fitzhenry & Whiteside Limited,
195 Allstate Parkway, Markham, Ontario L3R 4T8.

Library of Congress Cataloging-in-Publication Data
Bierds, Linda.
Heart and perimeter / by Linda Bierds.—1st ed.
p.   cm.
I. Title.
PS3552.I357H4   1991   91-8256
811'.54—dc20   CIP
ISBN 0-8050-1893-X
ISBN 0-8050-1765-8 (An Owl Book: pbk.)

Henry Holt books are available at special discounts
for bulk purchases for sales promotions, premiums,
fund-raising, or educational use. Special editions
or book excerpts can also be created to specification.
For details contact: Special Sales Director, Henry Holt and Company, Inc.,
115 West 18th Street, New York, New York 10011.

First Edition—1991

DESIGNED BY LUCY ALBANESE

Printed in the United States of America
Recognizing the importance of preserving the written word,
Henry Holt and Company, Inc., by policy, prints all of
its first editions on acid-free paper. ∞

1 3 5 7 9 10 8 6 4 2

1 3 5 7 9 10 8 6 4 2
pbk.

811.54
B

Grateful acknowledgment is made to the following magazines, where these poems first appeared: *The Atlantic* ("For the Sake of Retrieval"); *Field* ("And the Ship Sails On," "The Wind Tunnel"); *Indiana Review* ("From the Danube: 1829"); *The Journal* ("The Helmet of Mambrino," "Nancy Hanks Lincoln in Autumn: 1818," "The Running-Machines," "Winterreise, For Three Voices"); *The Kenyon Review* ("Audubon's Border Boy," "From Blakesware: Mary Lamb"); *The New England Review and Breadloaf Quarterly* ("April," "Yellow Chambers"); *The New Yorker* ("Bird in Space: First Study," "Träumerei," "The Grandsire Bells," "The Shakers," "White Bears: Tolstoy at Astapovo"); *Poetry Northwest* ("Halley's Bell," "Wanting Color," "Abundance"); *The Seattle Review* ("In the Beeyard").

I am grateful as well to the Ingram Merrill Foundation and the National Endowment for the Arts for grants that assisted me in completing this book.

To Sydney Kaplan

CONTENTS

• *This symbol is used to indicate a space between stanzas of a poem wherever such spaces are lost in pagination.*

PART ONE

THE SHAKERS

Picture a domino. A six perhaps, or placid
four. And resting upon it, like the grids in some
basement windows, three thin vertical lines.
This is a staff—for the dance notations of Rudolf Laban.
Torso twists, step turns and wrist folds,
gallops, jumps, all the motions
a body might make—in space, in time—
contractions, rotations, extensions, from head tilt
to the crook of the left thumb's outer segment,

spatter the staff in symbols. Black dots
and miniature boxcars, tiny rakes
for the fingers, double crosses for the knees,
the right ear's sickle, the eyebrow's mottled palette,
each intricate sketch on its half inch of grid line—
until a string of speckled rectangles

might tell us a foot was lifted,
set down at a slant on the metatarsus,
as a man might step down a path of loose stones.
In late-morning light, on the road to New Lebanon,
his elbow jumps with its bucket of lake bass.
Now and then, a whistle begins, spreads
into song, then the slack-cheeked slip into piety.

By midday his movements are rhythmic,
have become this dance passed down
through the centuries, then trapped in a patchwork

of labanotation. Two circles: one men, one women.
Stage left, a singer, a pulse of percussion.
The music begins and the circles are carriage wheels,
then closer—almost touching—are the black-specked wheels,
of a gear: one men, one women, in turn almost

touching, then the arms flung up in denial,
the bodies flung back into rippling lines,
fused, yet solitary, like a shoal of lake bass.
If there were lanterns then, they are lost here,
and smoke, the odors of sawdust, linseed.
But the costumes are true—white bibs and transparent
skullcaps, each foot in its column of black boot—

and the dancers strive with an equal devotion,
as if the feat of exact repetition were a kind of
eternity. Black dots and miniature boxcars.
Step here, they say, just here. And a foot is lifted,
a quick smile answers, This is enough, this striving—

daylight as it is with its sudden rain,
all the pockets of loose stones glistening.

FOR THE SAKE OF RETRIEVAL

As Whistler heard colors like a stretch of music—
long harmonies, violet to amber, double hummings of
silver, opal—so, in reverse, these three in their capsule,

free falling two hours through the black Atlantic, ears
popped, then filled with the music of Bach or Haydn,
might fashion a landscape. Low notes bring
a prairie perhaps, the sharps a smatter of flowers,
as the pip notes of sonar spring back to the screen
in little blossoms. They have come for the lost *Titanic*

and find instead, in the splayed beam of a headlamp,
silt fields, pale and singular, like the snow fields
of Newfoundland. On its one runner blade the capsule slides,
slips out through drift hummocks, through
stones the ice-age glaciers dropped, its trail
the foot-thin trail of a dancer, who
plants, glides, at his head the flurry

of a ship's chandelier, at his back a cinch-hook of icebergs
cast down through the winds of Newfoundland.
The music these three absorb
stops with the wreckage, with words
lipped up through a microphone:
flange, windlass, capstan, hull plating, then oddly, syllables
at a slant, as light might slant through window slats,

stairsteps, doorknob, serving bowl, teacup, Bordeaux.
Mechanical fingers, controlled by the strokes

of a joy stick, brush over debris, lifting, replacing.
In jittery strobe lights, camera lights, all colors
ground down to a quiet palette,
angles return, corners and spirals
pull back to the human eye—As if from some

iced and black-washed atmosphere, boiler coal,
a footboard and platter, each common shape
brightened, briefly held for the sake of retrieval.
The current spins silt like a sudden storm.
With the intricacy of a body the capsule adjusts,
temperature, pressure. Someone coughs, then the three

sit waiting, as in Whistler's *Sad Sea*
three are waiting. All around them are dollops
of winter wind, everywhere beach and sea. No horizon
at all in this painting, just a grey/brown thrum
beach to sea. How steady his breath must have been
on the canvas, his hands on the brushstrokes
of lap robes, of bonnets and beach chairs, the pull
of a red umbrella: each simple shape
loved and awash in the landscape.

THE HELMET OF MAMBRINO

Clarence King, 1842–1901

Am I not also of the family of Quixote, I wrote
and thought how a sentence might catch and slide
like a body's glissade from a snowy pinnacle.
A little breeze lifted the table-skirt
and for a few moments, all my glissades
came skimming—head back, legs cocked
like the fore-beams of sleighs, my geologist's knapsack
clapped over my heart. How the thin air
seemed to thicken in those moments from slope
to lake bed, snow field to rubble, as each summit

slipped back to its wedge of sky. Whitney.
Shasta. Tyndall, the first I would witness:
brief harmony, brief melding of truth and illusion.
We had carried our blankets curled into knapsacks,
knobby with venison and pocket-levels, cooked beans,
compasses, in from the west, then up, up,
past glacier blocks, past the cries of martens, high
and sharp, like the ripping of silk.
With the slack-limbed swings of a boy, my companion
pulled to the summit, felt a second's triumph, then

stopped: just to the east was a parallel range,
higher, so close it might be reflection. . . .

I would know that tumble often, that
explorer's slide, belief to belief, conviction
to its memory, to conviction. Once I placed
my marker-coin on Mt. Whitney's double, lost in a mist,

convinced I had climbed to the highest land. Once
I charted a lake from opal air. And loved
its ripplings, although there were none, and its false
crescent of shoreline. As Quixote loved brass
as if it were gold, a green-stroked barber's bowl
in the roadway, as if it were dropped armor.
His misjudgments, my misjudgments—not from errors
so much as attractions, thin-aired, brief enchantments. . . .

With slack-limbed swings my companion descended,
not homeward, but east, down through the gorge wall.
I mimicked his toe holds, or held his weight
on a stretch of rope, as he did mine, body
over body, until a slim valley welcomed us,
as a funnel base might welcome drifting silt.
All afternoon, a thick shade followed our footprints.
Wrapped in blankets on the valley floor, we watched
as it climbed the eastern wall, until only

those peaks held sunlight, then their clouds, then
nothing. Moonlight began, down over the gorge wall,
repeating our path and the shade's path, as if
we were currents, as if we were winds
in a capped bowl. The temperature dropped. Slowly
the snow congealed. Mist on the planes of granite
slicked, congealed. We watched as the brooks
stopped in their patterns, as the rhythmic clickings
of waterfalls stopped. And the last drops
on the blanket's edge, and the last drops

on the boot cuffs. We would not sleep
but wait, enchanted, as half-foot by
half-foot a silence curled through,

west to east. Then we packed and set out, convinced
we had witnessed a certain death, even as the sun rose.

RINGING

This thimble one, with a lentil clapper.
This one of shell.
These top-notched ones, for the harnesses of horses.
And these, for the fist-shaped, candle-spun
carousels of children. This one of the pear-shape,
this of the tulip, the fish mouth, the pomegranate,
the beehive. This room-sized one, stung
by four men in black braids, their arms
underhanding a muted log, in unison,
underhanding, casting the sanded log-tip
to the lotus-etched sweet-spot of the bell,
then again, underhanding in unison, like
the casters of waterbuckets, the ring and the splay,

and slowly, the child closes her book. A sound
has begun, just out from the window. A tap-scratch,
thwirr. Some rabbit, perhaps, trapped
in a shallow snare, great hind feet
plucking tufts from the crabgrass. She rises,
sits back in her soft chair, rises. Perhaps she will
witness a certain death, but the shelter of the book
is a memory now, the path to the window
infinite, nothing, as she steps, stalls, steps, then
slips shoulder first to the waxy pane—and there
is her brother in the orchard below, casting stones
with a sling through the dense, brittle leaves
of the sugar maples. No targets at all there, no prey—

his small head tipped and attentive—just the pull,
release, then long after, the answerings.

THE LOST FELICE

For wine, they drank the ocean . . . .
Marsden Hartley

Three crows are side-stepping a ligature of wire
on a backdrop white as your hallow shirt.

It is morning.
The radio crackles, then fastens a down-pull
to the strands of Schubert's "Winterreise," as its hero
follows through a pathway of songs
not his lover so much as his longing.

Another tooth lost today, sucked up from the gum
with the sound of a spoon from the tapioca.
But the apples have softened in their wash
of hot brine, and the Whitney
has taken *The Old Bars*. Fever-blanched,

Schubert died with hemorrhages
swelling up to the skin, not unlike your own drowning,
sea water plumping the smallest depressions.

I am deaf now, and the voice of the tenor
or long violin is fractured—a continuance, of course,
but segmented, like a spine, or
the chaos of bell buoys in an autumn storm.

I troubled the beach for twelve days.

Last night in a dream, you walked out
of the sea with a speckling

and the first bloodless paper cuts of gill.
I will carry that secret to *The Lost Felice*:

black oilskins, sou'wester, your hand in the foreground.
And from the fingers—growing down
from the knuckles and nail-tips—the bodies of

mackerels. A continuance, of sorts.
And a rendering: apples, to the wash, to
the pulp and brine-white absences of morning.

———

WINTERREISE,
FOR THREE VOICES

homage to Hawthorne Gray
b. 1889
d. stratosphere balloon flight, 1927

Is there no place for me above ground?
                            Franz Schubert

1.

Up through the boosters and crystals,
through the boxy brick
and static-free stations
of Louisville, Springfield,
the music came.
Through the rooftops and cloudbanks,
to the pin-thick tip
of the trailing wire.
Through the basket, through
the sixty pounds of outerwear—
fleece and steerhide—
to the ear, to the voice
that offered in the freezing air
its own balloon, steam-plumped
and resonant.

At ten thousand feet, "Kashmiri."
At twenty, Schumann's "Träumerei." Then
"Thinking of You" and "After the Ball."
Then, in the flat-palmed slap
of a ballast cap, the wire wrenched

free, the music ended. . . .

2.

It lifts, falls a bit, lifts. Like
a bell ringer's body!

The symptoms of rickets were upon me.
And ice, at the glove seams and nostrils.
What can I tell you? Eight miles

turned the legs into water. A warming,
of sorts, in the stratosphere. (Which is
nothing, not even the seam line
of fog on a river.)

And the balance of ballast and speed is
intricate, like the sea-cups
of inner ears. Mine filled, released, then
stalled, sucked down into pellets of corn.

Still, the thwirr, thwirr of the neck flap
gives a kind of singing. . .

3.

"From a string-swung pattern of chalk on the floor,
cut silk into gores, crawling out on each thin,
equilateral leg—sixty, seventy, one hundred feet—
snipping and smoothing. Then stitch
the sectors with lap-over edges, varnish
the stitch marks, the tapering webbings,
hand sand and varnish the hoop ring—

each layer of first-growth, hardwood girth
stroked, sanded, stroked, sanded,
until a rider below might see in reflection,
goggles, cap, a ripple of shoulder. . ."

4.

. . . Some giddiness affects me.
And the ghost shapes of

strawberries! I welcome their curves
and puckerings, their slope
to a dropped apex.

No air left, I fear. No ballast

to cast past a plummet.

You must cushion the clock against freezing.
The instep and toes.

What can I tell you?
It moves with the wind, so
there is no wind.

5.

. . . "Hand cut and varnish the tip valve,
neck ring, braid and knot the balloon net,
valve line, car lines, leading lines,

taking care for a perfect harmony, balance,
that the rider may sense no rising at all,
but a slowly receding world."

6.

... And began again in the hum
of the neck flap, the snare-scratch of wicker.
Then followed the long descent, one hour, two, until
by night the basket skimmed at last
the fence and shrub lines of eastern
Tennessee, brushed over the outbuildings, rooftops,
the sleepers inside their wooden houses

hearing nothing, just a scratch and branch rustle
as one black oak on a hill of oaks
was entered, filled, the envelope settling
like a silk shawl, then the round crest of the tree
flickering silver, yellow, in the morning sun,
its billow and fresh tendrils
asking, for an instant, the first risers
what quick spring now occupied
the landscape, the new day.

APRIL

A little wind. One creak from a field crow.
And the plow rips a shallow furrow, hobbles
from guide-stake to guide-stake,
draws its first contour line,
and parallel, its next, next,
then the turn-strips and deadfurrows, the headlands
and buffer lines, until the earth from a crow's vantage
takes the pattern of a fingertip.

And by noon the shadows are gridways: cut soil,
the man on the plow, the plow and simple tail,
each squat on a stretch of slender shade,
black and grid-straight, like the line of anti-light

a screen clicks up to, before its image
swells, deepens. Dark glass
going green, in the shade-darkened room
of a laboratory—it casts a little blush
across the face there, the shoulders and white pocket,
then magnifies the moon-skin of a microbe, then deeper,
electron molecules in a beam so stark it smolders.

The man on the plow fears frost,
its black cancer. The man at the screen
fears the storm an atom renders
on the lattice of a crystal. And heat. And the slick
back-licks of vapor. With luck, with the patience
the invisible nurtures, he will reshape
•

frost-making microbes, snip frost-hook genes
with a knife of enzymes. And at thirty degrees,
twenty, through seam lines of snap beans, oranges,
almonds, potatoes, no frost will form, no ratchet-bite
of ice, all the buds of transformed microbes
blossoming, reblossoming, like the first flowers.

There is wind at the rim of the black-out shade.
One tick of the focus gears. Another. On a glass plate,
enlarged from nothing to filaments, the lines
of DNA wander, parallel, in tandem,
curled together past pigment blips, resin,
as the contour lines for autumn oranges
swerve in unison past boulder pods. The light

through the mottled skins of genes
is not light at all, but friction, caught and channeled,
like pigment caught in the scratch-marks of caves.
This was our world, the marks say: horse, maize,
vast gods drawn down to a palm print.
Drawn up from nothing the microbes gather,
a little wind on the curtain,
sun on the curtain's faded side, on the crow and plow,
on the earth sketched perfectly to receive it.

AND THE SHIP SAILS ON

Federico Fellini, *Cinecittà*

One pull on the plastic sea
and it's 1914. A man stands, draped
in a drop cloth of ripples. On his forehead,
fan wind. On his scalp, the glow of a latex moon.
Again, he thinks, and again the tug
and sea shudder, the camera's gill-flap snout
slipping out past his shoulder.

It is a filming of artifice and, hence, an elegy,
each prop in memoriam to its lost
correspondent, each scene indoors—
So that nothing is captured but its monument.
Foam clouds. In memoriam. Grease paint
and frippery. The ship itself

strung out like vertebrae over nine sound stages.
With the flick of his wrists the decades drop,
the 1914 churned Atlantic
returns in a plastic shimmer, frail
and arid, its centuries of plankton and blind fish

reduced to a glisten at the fingertips.
Then he straightens, waits, and here
is the lunch cart's thick perfume,
someone's arm at his elbow.

∾

So it continues. Waiting. A little action,
silence. Years pass and their flip-frame echoes—
in memoriam—and now he will read

that a thought has been pictured.
Midmorning, dappled sun on the pages,
and there, in fuchsia and blue,
a thought's first picture: two loops
at the ends of a needle.

A primate, he reads, wrapped in a halo of wires.
To its left, a handle. In its buff, flesh-petal ear,
Again. And just before pulling,
through the milliseconds of cell snap and fire,
through the wires and inky dot-strewn pictures,
the thought of pulling: loop, and then loop.
And looking remarkably, he thinks,
like a child's thumb-sized ship,

walnut-half for a hull, needle mast,
an ash leaf perhaps, twice-pierced
to a constant billow: flying jib, spinnaker,
topgallant, main skysail, or the dark
frigate's fluttering royals, urged on by the wind
or the wind's correspondent.

IN THE BEEYARD

Clover-rich, lugged close to the thorax and twirring heart,
wax-capped, extracted, the viscid liquid
is not gold at all, but the color of cellophane, ice.
A little heat and its sugars may darken,
emerge, as fingerprints rise through a dusting of talcum,

but there in the dry-packed winter beehives
it is clear, the complex nothing of air or water.
And warm—although the orchard outside has slowly chilled,
snow on the windbreak, deep snow on the hives
in their black jackets. The honey is warm,
and the hive walls, and the domes of bearded wheat straw
tucked under tarpaper rooflines.

To nurture this tropic climate, the bees
have fashioned a plump wheel, clustered body to body
on honey cells, chests clicking out a friction, a heat—
faster, slower, in inverse proportion
to the day's chill—while the hives
keep a stable ninety degrees, warm-blooded

as the keepers who cross through the beeyard.
They move with the high-steps of waders, a man,
his daughter. He clears blown snow from the hive doors.
She lowers her ear to the deep hummings.
Like mummies, she thinks of the cloaked rows, like
ghosts. Then salt pillars, headless horsemen
turned white by some stark moonlight.
In a flurry the images reach her,

·

their speed almost frightening, splendid,
as if the myths and fables of her life are a blizzard
drawn suddenly to her, drawn suddenly visible
through some brief interaction of
temperature, light. And the day itself then
swells a half-step closer: the sky and knotted
peach trees, her father's thick form

smelling slightly of bacon. He turns
and a bowed ear blooms, backlit a moment
by the sudden sunlight, little veins and spiderings
plum-colored, then fuchsia, as a warmth spreads
over his face, her shoulders, over the windbreak
and hive doors. She opens her jacket and soft liner.
The bees, in their perfect circle, still.

FROM THE DANUBE: 1829

He nods as the boat slaps west, the river, east,
its high left bank and shrunken right
asymmetrical as his shaved skull. Half the scalp hair gone!
Half the moustache and beard—and deep in the prison courtyard,
his head cast the shadow of a nautilus, long spiral
spilling out at the top. Now a cap hides the past,

hides the midday sunlight creeping over the deck rails.
When it warms his left ear, his cheek and stubbled half-beard,
he departs, walks north through willow brakes, then
the milky stalks of spring rye. A little song begins
just under his breastbone, soon an answering grief.
Like the struggles of his princes a wind wells up, troubling
the rye fields, plucking chaff to a random foam.
And then it is all dropped back, as he has been,

plucked then dropped back to this simple path.
Far ahead, clouds turn in unison, at their borders
two field hawks, and at last they are joined
by a strand of smoke swept up from his cottage rooftop.
Dark loaves, perhaps, or the purple thighs of brush drakes
spitting their juice through the firebox. And above them,
his wife in her nubbled stockings, her long forearm
thrust deep in the oven chamber, testing the temperature
by tolerance: five counts for fowl, four for hare, two
for the spongy hearts of rye bread. When she straightens

he is with her, stopped in the doorway, cap and rucksack
slack on the floorboards, his rough laugh

sharp and finite, like hooves over bricks.
God's jesters, she smiles, looking first
to his hairline, then down to her reddened arm,
its years of solitary duty
glazing the skin to the gleam of bottomfish.

That evening they walk to the beet fields, through acres
of early shoots, spaced and rippling, like the tassels
of horse soldiers. He tells of a flood near Ostrov, how
the river swelled to a gold bay, studded with rooftops.
Soon he moves from the chaos of water, to the chaos

of stars. To the problem of a candle in a sudden wind,
it solid flame scattered, dropped back. His eyes cannot leave
the waxing moon—all night they move past
its glowing half-face, rest on the darker other,
where, in the scud and flush of new-growth light,
all the ghosts are forming.

FROM BLAKESWARE:
MARY LAMB

It is the plum-light of dawn—that flush
like a thumb on the eyelid—
and the madness that approaches me
carries two dappled coins:

We vacationed in a ghost house.

From a flurry like the chaos in a candlesnuff
I ended my mother's life.

The second you remember. It rolls before me
down the narrow walkways.
The first is the mansion of our childhood,

∿

Blakesware:

marble busts and tapestried wainscots,
mosaics nubbled like the elbows
of dowagers. Long dead. The mansion
left empty for years, its only revivers
Charles, myself, our grandmother curled to her

caretaker's duties. Wind seeped past the doorframes
and hem lines. We roamed the halls as
visitors, conquerors, placed warm cheeks
on the marble faces. Guests. And not—
our shared heritage that seam line,

cheek line, that gradual melding of
warmth and cold.

Middays we sat in the orangery,
Charles with his head on my worsted lap, I
with my bodice pouch of leaf-shaped marzipan.
The odor of citrus slipped down from the trees,
sharp and immaculate, like the scent
from a surgeon's handbowl. And the alpine dam
brushed over the split limes, the skin
of her bloated udder

∿

shifting like my mother's coarse chemise,
the breasts beneath in watery moons,

the moon itself already at the window. A longing
has risen all day, cool and infinite,
like the flesh of peaches. My mother scolded.
Just outside the window, the black gate hook
closed over its prong. I remember. TAP, just
TAP, then a knife entered my mother's heart.

I remember. A longing. A flurry.
My elbow bent

∿

then tap, the shuttlecock veered from the battledore,
looped through the courtyard nursery,
its spars and patchy barbules
dropping a season's dust, catching it back
on the low return. To my left,
the mosaics of fawns. Behind Charles,

pillows, a sloped divan
dimpled from the torsos of children. These
were our rituals: to replace the shuttlecock
on its ring of feather crumbs. Exactly.
To place our bodies where their bodies lounged,
to fill the impressions, exactly. Something
settling, something lifting to meet it. Two worlds
and a seam line, thin, barely visible, like
the distance from madness to longing.

We are human. Sometimes wretched. Sometimes

∿

forgiven. Each day in my brother's house
I stitch the simple seams of mantuas.
Now and then, two coins are offered. One
you remember: the moon, of course, its planes
and dapplings. The other begins

as a hoofprint in winter. A light snow
has covered the orangery. The alpine dam steps

out down the carriage path, each print an alliance
of light and dark: snow, the black stones
of our earth. As she walks her lungs
offer ovals of steam. They lift with the rhythm
of breathing—past my neckline,
the curve of my ear.

WHITE BEARS:
TOLSTOY AT ASTAPOVO

The wheels of the train were a runner's heartbeat—
systole, diastole, the hiss-tic of stasis—
as they flipped through the scrub trees and autumn grasses,
slowing at last at the station lamps.
And perhaps the fever had carried this memory,
or the journey, or, just ahead in the darkness,
the white, plump columns of lamplight.

He is five, six, locked at the center
of the evening's first parlor game:
*Go stand in a corner, Lyova, until you stop thinking
of a white bear.* To his left
there is pipe smoke. Behind him
a little laughter from the handkerchiefs.
And in his mind, white fur
like the blizzards of Tula! He studies the wall cloth
of vernal grass and asters, a buff stocking, trouser cuff,
but just at the rescue of a spinet bench
two claws scratch back. A tooth. Then
the lavender palate of polar bears.

I cannot forget it, he whispers. And would not,
through the decades that followed—
the white, cumbersome shape
swelling back, settling, at the rustling close
of an orchard gate, or the close
of a thousand pen-stroked pages,

white bear, in the swirls of warm mare's milk,
at the side of the eye. White bear,

when his listless, blustery, aristocratic life
disentangled itself, landlord to
shoemaker, on his back a tunic, in his lap
a boot, white bear, just then,
when his last, awl-steered, hammer-tapped peg
bit the last quarter sole.

In the gaps between curtains. And now,
in the lamp-brightened gaps between fence slats,
there and there, as if the bear
were lurching at the train's slow pace,
and behind it—he was certain—the stifling life he fled
rushing to meet him: family, servants, copyrights,
just over the hill in the birch trees.
Simplicity. He sighed. Dispossession.
A monastery, perhaps. Kasha in oil. At eighty-two
his body erased to the leaf-scrape of sandals.
And even the room near the station, the small bed
with its white haunch of pillow,

even the mattress, where he shivered
with fever or a train's slow crossing, and whispered,
and, just before morning, died,
was better. Deep autumn. Already the snows
had begun in the foothills, erasing
the furrows and scrub trunks, erasing at last
the trees themselves, and the brooks,
and the V-shaped canyons the brooks whittled.

There and there, the landscape no more
than an outreach of sky, a swelling, perhaps,
where an orchard waited, then boundary posts, fence wire,
then, below, the lavender grin of the clover.

NANCY HANKS LINCOLN IN AUTUMN: 1818

Thirst. And the slow pains of the stomach.
Her heart gives the sound of an oar through water, blunt
and diminishing, or the slipping of hooves over oak roots.

No window in view, yet the door near her bed
frames the nut trees and sycamores, the cows
folded down in a clearing. Like an alchemist's mark
for infinity—loop beside loop, horizontal eight—
each body curls back to itself: shoulder arched, neck dipped, head
stretched back to rest on a circle of hip.

Their milk will kill her, their journeys down game paths
to the white, forest blossoms of snake-root.
Bud high with poison the vine plants rushed,
muzzle, to milk vein, to udder, to a thirst
whose final magnification seems a form of mockery.

An ax claps somewhere to her left. The table
with its belly of puncheon casts the shadow of a ferry,
as if the floor were again the flat Ohio,
Kentucky behind, Indiana just ahead in a chaos of trees.
Someone coughed then, she remembers. Sharp coughs,
skittering. Someone sang of the journey the soul

must make, little boat over water. Their home
took the color of chestnuts. She read aloud
from the fables of Aesop: foxes and eagles. The crow
and the pitcher—its water out of reach,
just off from the tongue, his beak at the rim

like ax strokes. To her left they are chopping,
then whittling a clearing with fire. They are stacking
ripped vines, saplings, and underbrush
like a plump wreath at the base of a sycamore.
It will burn in an arc-shaped heart, huge
and magnificent, dark veins of heat
rippling off at the edges. Will the birds break again then

out from the trees? The passenger pigeons and parakeets
lift as they have in a thick unit, their thousand bodies
dragging the shadow of a wide pond

down over the game paths, down over the oak trees
and cattle, the doorframe, bedposts, cupped hands,
bellows, the cheese in its muslin napkin?
Until shape after darkened shape floats in a wash of air?

Thirst. Braiding every thought back to an absence.
She drinks from her cup. Drinks again. On a hillside
the children are laughing, called out from their sorrow
by the spectacle of flames. Or by birds
in a sudden jumble, perhaps. Or the placid cows
catching handkerchiefs of ash on their broad faces.
How simply two circles can yield to each other,

curl back to each other without ending:
Raised shoulder, a dipping, raised hip.
The path an oar makes in water, in air, then in water.

PART TWO

PART TWO

HALLEY'S BELL

from the diary of Marc Brunel

This morning gave quince meat, a tangle
of duck eggs. And the sickly half luminance
of a candle flame in daylight.

We have tunneled the Thames, Rotherhithe to Wapping.
Eighteen years, the lights each day of two hundred candles
swelling and withering in the shaft wind.

Picture forceps clamped over a honeycomb.
That was my digging shield: the head prong
holding the river up, the foot prong
delaying the drop into Hades. And between, lodged
in each chamber, one miner, one shovel.

It crept through the clay
like the steadfast orbit of Jupiter.
Each season December, each hour a 4 P.M. umber.
Loaded as we are with the weight of the river,
I wrote, *we push forth our shield, walk*

our frames outward to three hundred feet.
And feasted there, now and then. Wet walls,
the candle-thrown shadows of forks and miners.
And music, sometimes—near the table's north end—the band
of His Majesty's Coldstream Guards, or a single clarinet,
its resonance snaking from mouthpiece to body, through
the end-stopped body of the tunnel.

Fevers began. And the blindnesses—gradual—
like the inchmeal closures of lantern flames.

Five times the river irrupted, each influx predicted
by a pick-axed flash of boot buckles,
of hammer heads, jawbones, rag bolts—whatever
the riverbed nestled—rushing past us with the silt.

The heads give way from the moment the legs do!
But remain with the frames. And like the shoes hold—
the great feet bear up the push of the in-tide.

In a diving bell drawn from the blueprints of Halley,
my son would visit each breach, sit on the dome bench
at the absolute standoff of worlds: water and air in equal
resistance. At the glass-slick lip of the bell, he told me,
is a shield made perfect by the elements,
by the irrefutable theorem of

pressing back. There is wind now, just over
the hedgerows, and the ratchet of the milk cart.
With a telescope, my son returns from a night
in the meadow, walking toward me
through the chattering galaxy of the linden trees.

The shoes, I wrote, *our security rests in the shoes.*

LIGHT, STEAM

Meriwether Lewis, 1774–1809

Because the mockingbird offered its own clear song,
he was told, someone would die. Someone who caught
the pared-down crystalline trill
like a quick wind in the ear cup, the simplified song
strung out at that moment, tree limb, to river,
to the curved backs of his countrymen
pushing their keelboat through the grip of a riffle.

And yet no one. So they continued, westward. Folklore,
he thought, or perhaps the bird was its own victim,
earth-whittled, erased to a filament of sound.
He filled his lungs, called everything in: wild artichoke,

lamb's-quarter, sand rush, wild cucumber. Squirrels
swam the Missouri with the scratch-marks of leaves.
By June the cliff-works began: soft sandstone,
rain- and wave-cut, two hundred, three hundred
perpendicular feet, edging the river path like buildings.
Long galleries, he wrote, white parapets
silent with statuary. A city, if he wished. A culture:
by a fixed slant of the eye, his culture,
swung round to meet him. As if for those miles,
stretched back in the flat pirogue,
he were the apex of a certain history—in his wake,
wild artichokes, white buildings in a half-strip of sunlight.

∾

Then the mountains were reached. Then the sea.
Then, in the half-light repetition renders, the long

turning back began, bootprint to bootprint. And for him—
having charted and claimed, having placed on the grasses
and landscape the syllables of his time—the long
returning: Cascades slipped back
to their borders of clouds, the Bitterroots, Lolo Pass,
the crest of the continent's peaked divide,
returned, slipped back, while in from the east,
the thick applause that welcomed his journey
swelled and tapered like a slow exhale.

No sleep. Again, no sleep. I have held the expedition,
he wrote, in equal estimation
with my own existence. And inseparable
from his own existence, each bootprint a memory,
each memory a cell in a layering of cells:
all the years of his life, water, wind,
the arc-shapes of language and saddlehorns,
childhood combs, history, flute notes, lamb's-quarter,
cool drams of persimmon brandy, gathering within him.

And now slowly withdrawing. No sleep, delirium,
the latticed borders of self, other, dissolving, pulling back.
And what at the center then, stark and horrific?
Tiny gnarl-root of light? Steam?

He stepped from the swale of the Natchez Trace,
down through a tangle of oaks and maples,
to the peg- and sod-clogged dogtrot
of an L-shaped inn. All evening, the October air
grew thicker, birdsong like a border to his own voice

as he spoke in the words of a president, a pauper,
alone, pacing out and back through his small room,
spoke in the words of a diplomat, child, each voice
the echo of a common errand, that
carrying outward of their shared voice.

Delirious, someone said. Then a silence.
Two shots, and then after, a little scratching,
as a gourd scraped down through a wooden bucket.

∾

Water, he said. It was witnessed. Pale filament
of sound. As if, irrevocably lost, wanting at last
to leave the body, he wanted in turn to replenish it.
Simple word, like a heartbeat, then the gourd-scratch

like the scraping of bird claws on a dry branch.
Beak open, sharp tongue pulled back from a note's completion.
To the left of its head a blackberry hangs, plump
and dew-covered, each chamber a globe, each chamber
a world where the song is traveling.

FOR IVAN DOIG

TRÄUMEREI

All I have done in music seems a dream
I can almost imagine to have been real.
Robert Schumann, 1810–1856

Perhaps this, then: the holystone licks
of the winter Rhine. A cleansing.
A scouring away. Anything to free him
from the constant filling.

Weeping, in slippers and dark robe, maddened
by phantom voices, music,
he walks from his house with
the tentative half-steps of a pheasant.
A little rain collects on his robe hem,
and street meal, the cubiform dust-chips
of cobblestones. He has carried no coin purse
and offers to the bridge guard
a silk face cloth, then the image
of a man in bedclothes, in the quarter-arc of flight

from railing to river.
There is wind—upward—
and the parallel slaps of his slippers.
With the abrupt closure of a trumpet mute
his heart stops. Then the music, voices. Water
has flushed through his robe sleeves, and
the thin, peppered trenches
between groin and thigh.

He will surface
as an opal surfaces: one

round-shouldered curve of brocade in the wave-chop.
Then his heart kicking back.
And the oarlocks of rowers who are
dipping to save him?
A-notes and A-notes—perfect—in unison.

∿

What else but to starve?
The starched coats of asylum guards
give a fife's chirrups. They are joined by
tintinnabulum, chorus and oboe
on his brief walks to the ice baths.

At the first flat shocks and frigid clearings
he smiles, murmurs
that his madness is at least his love,
distorted, of course, pervasive, but still . . .
aural. A music. The trees

by the fenceline fill, release. One year,
two. He follows halfway, taking
into the self the quarter-notes of
footsteps, the cacophony of laughter, wagons, doors,
the hums of the candle-snuff.
Writing stops, then speech. No word,
no flagged dot on its spidery stave
to diminish the filling. What else but

.

to turn from all food, to decrease from without
like the August peaches? To take at the last
the fine, unwavering balance
of an arc—heart and perimeter—
a cup where all sound resonates? . . .

A bell has fallen in Moscow, he once wrote,
so huge it carried its belfry to the ground.
And into the ground. The bell lip
and shoulder boring deep in the earth. Then
a cross-rip of belfry. Then, through
the stark reversal of summer grasses,
four pale steps leading down.

ABUNDANCE

Tom Thumb, circa 1880

Bronze plums on the spaniel-high table
have called back his wedding: the gift of goblets,
tusk-ware, and from Lincoln
the ink-black and mackerel stretches of
Chinese fire screens. The day attended

by two thousand—the decades that followed
attended by thousands, elbow thrusts and huzzas,
the brays of Barnum's calliopes—
and we are God's jesters, Lincoln said,
the long and the short of it.

This evening brought a snowfall to the waist
and fireplace flames draw steam
from his boot soles—heel and shank
in the breadth of a silver dollar. Through the rose
and marigold tones of the screen's floral lacquer

float the undersides of pigeons, steam phantoms,
one upon one in a thin wall. An abundance,
Lincoln told him. Making black
of the blue Indiana sky. Or a sunset, he thinks now:
in appropriate light, the rose undersides of
six million passenger pigeons
pulling up a stratum of sunset

thin and shivering, like the backdrop washes
in the paintings of Haydon. Tea has begun,
its steep and blossoming. *Long bullets are drawing*

the birds to extinction, he reads in the firelight.
All the hunters with hay carts. And isn't it

humanness, he wonders, to pare back the abundant,
the threatening excessive? Humanness—elbow thrusts,
huzzas—to exalt the contained? To glad-hand
the palm-sized shoulders, push a breast
to the tiny chest, to kiss and kiss the cheek pouch
until a rash with the down of strawberries rises?

They darkened the sky. One flock two hours
in passing. He turns. In the bronze plating of plums
rests a fish scale teapot. . . .

From his wedding, he walked with his miniature bride
through the White House, the portico and hallways,
to the infinite dome of the Blue Room.
Lincoln rose to greet them like a gathering storm,
black hair, black beard, black shoulders,
the reach of his black sleeves.

THE RABBIT

I am going to Sakhalin,
but not for the convicts.
                    Chekhov

Snow to the window ledge, and the haystack beyond
begins at its apex, the lime trees
at the bronchial splay of their branches.

I am fit today. Fused, in the sense
of replacement, the well for the worn. You ask me
for images of Sakhalin. Think of globes,
black or white. The round lobes of the island,
the shaved skulls of its convicts—half the head hair gone,
half remaining, like a border of westerly clouds.

And flames, perpetual: the spontaneous fires of forests.
By night they were gothic, by day
just a haze through the scrapes of potato knives.

There was scurvy, weeping, and a greed
for the poisons of wolfsbane. I went, I am certain,
not so much for my census of exiles,
or for medicine, literature, but for the infinite power

of departure. Such ice now. A storm from the west,
I am told, is coating the great bells: for each,
at the west, a quarter-sheath of snow.

By morning they cough and revive.
•

My lungs carry hatch-lines of infection, thin
and circular, like the carmine lashes of whores.
Or flame-tips, of course, over pulpy islands.

At night, buoyed by snow, attracted by light,
a rabbit visits my window, straining up
with her paws past the first pane. Bi-ocular,
she may see me at first as two, then,
through some steadfast interior shuffling,
one. Fused, perhaps, in the sense
of replacement. As, in this increasingly
weather-locked room, she for me—
white arc-shape of undercoat—replaces
the moon and its tributaries.

WANTING COLOR

Sergei Prokudin-Gorskii

The day is blue and well appointed,
the windless stillness of stone. And Be stone as well,
I tell her. For five seconds, six.
The distance of a sneeze through the plume grass.

It is a flax farm in Perm, 1909. Through the windowframe
of my camera, a woman in the pinafore of her ancestors
stands at a flax-break. The wooden blade in her hand
and the flax jutting down from the sawhorse break

mimic a gesture that in fact is solid,
stalled in its tumbling like
a stream in the winter Urals.

Wanting color, I have fashioned a spectrum box:
three filters—cyan, magenta, yellow—
three shutter-clicks in the distance of a sneeze,
then three separations placed
over one another, like the notes of an A-chord,

and the world is as clear—focused—
as the crow to my left
troubling the hens for a pearl of grain.
Should it step through our still scene, I tell her,
its passage would fracture, a languid stretch
become first a blossom, then on examination

three petals of wing: extension, pause, retraction.
A disquietude stirs in the cities, ripples out
through the rail lines like

•

a stretched wing. Using color, the slowest motion
will fracture, I tell her. Rivers, windblown clouds
and groundcover. A monk peeking toward me
from potato fields near Svetlista
made a halo of his canon hat and neck curls.
And once from the framework of a bell tower
I focused and a soldier on the street below
walked out of himself through three
greatcoats: cyan, magenta, yellow.

There is a fusion that is stillness. And a meadow
in the insistence of a river! In service to the Tsar
I have captured the clarity of mosques,
of bridges, salt mines, semaphore signals. A fear

has begun within me. A kernel yet,
but growing, like the achievements of

a spectrum box. On the village cathedrals
there are onion domes the green of juvenile wheat.
Often it is startling, how in motion we break

to the primaries. And Be still now, I tell her. Now.
Still. And here are the shutter's scissor-click closures
like the crow's beak over pellets of grain.
At the side of my eye it is lifting, neck stretched
in elation, then the solemn hinge of the underbeak,
the plucked seeds already opening.

THE WIND TUNNEL

Wilbur Wright, 1867–1912

The oysters, perhaps. Or the simple milk.
Then rod-shaped bacillus speckling the stomach,
the slow typhoid blooming in rose spots.
They wither to the circles coins
might offer. On the chest, the eyelids.

There will be no recovery. Each clear day
bends to delirium. By evening,
the amber pitcher at rest on the bedstead
is a face from the first triumph: sand-pocked,
exuberant, here and there, a smatter of beads
with the glisten of fan oil.

Has the wind begun? In the chimney
and sycamores, in the flat belly of the kettle?
We fashioned a tunnel in the shape
of Orion, wide at the shoulders
and tapering. Six feet of pine and a little window
where the miniature wings were watched. A fan
pushed the breeze through a honeycomb grid
and the wings, with their muslin and silk,
spruce spars and wire, their camber, warp, drift, drag,

rustled. A man could ride there, were the scene
enlarged. Head first in the grace
of a shallow dive, strapped to the wing spine.
All speed a sound, then, all distance a pressure
on the lips, eyelids—the lurch and shudder of climbing,
soaring, yet the same flat patch of Ohio soil

•

locked underneath. Humus and grain dust.
And the evening, has it begun yet? Pale wine,
a dozen oysters, each fat in its dollop
of milky sea? The sound the planes made,
dropping in from the sea at Kitty Hawk,
dropping into the pumice troughs
of sand dunes, was the sound of tape
peeled back from a canker, or
the rasp-strokes of air

through the honeycomb grid of a tunnel.
He could ride there. The great wind—
like the wind of flying—erasing
his cough, his swallow, erasing
at last the senses themselves.
Smoke. The deep kite tails of color. Ice. Silk.
The little song at the brain stem, the little word—

and yet nothing—nothing—no travel at all:
flat Ohio, the rocker and amber pitcher
fixed at his side.

YELLOW CHAMBERS

Great cells, twenty, forty yards long,
like the masterworks of bees. Each circled a reach
of helium, nitrogen, and the soft-sided
airship lifted.

It was the mole year of war.
On the Oregon coast we found nothing, floating
for days near the plate of our shadow.
Not plane, not ship, some hushed, lumbering
other. And our seascape that winter?
Twin slates and a seam line.

We sounded for hulls, studied the surface
for lace-work cavitation. No blip. No
burble. Studied for fins, gull-fluff,
the white caps and clouds riffling—
above us, the great lung of the envelope
filling, releasing. On the fourth morning,

a thread of warm gelatin worked
through our veins, all of our gestures softening.

Not here, we said, not there. Floating
and not, like mites on a pelican. And each night,
a mile inland, the shoreline there, not there,
as black-out curtains condensed the light,
patted it down to one yellow chamber, then
another, another, then our own:
cot, galley, a pouch of soft apples.

.

Behind darkened portholes, we cupped
to the sonar like a shared sense, the last nights,
lowered the globe of the hydrophone
and listened to the whales trill. The braided cable
reached into the sea—its flurry

of gill-sloosh and beak-clicks, its rattles,
birrs, rasps, whistles—like the rope
I had followed as a boy, hand
over hand from the house to the stable:
deep winter, four feet of snow,
the days still snowing. No up or down, then,
sky and pasture a single disk.
I would pass by rope from the house

to its memory, toward the yellow memory
of the stable: timothy, the oil-scent of horses.
At the creak of the door-glide their faces
turned toward me. Fourteen, in unison—
one movement, one motion—the way wind
might cross through wide leaves.

THE RUNNING-MACHINES

They were bicycles without chains, without
pedals or sprocket gears, or the V-shaped alliance
of seat tube and down tube. Two wheels,
of course—leader and acolyte—a saddle, luggage rack,
now and then, an S-curve of lantern hook. And their riders

were runners. Propped on the saddles, feet
on the ground, forearms braced by a shelf
at the handlebars, they leaned forward, pushed off into
trots, then the stiff-legged canters of ostriches.
Goethe saw them on the field grounds
of the Paradies, a sorcerer's swarm of motion and light,
and the blue-eyed coachmen of the Mayor of Haarlem
watched as he stroked past the bulb fields,
taking speed on a slope toward the Zuider Zee,

and dreaming, through each wheel-rutted chatter
in his spine, of the perfect track, the downhill, gallopless
soaring of racers. Legs lifted, held, they will stream
through the Tivoli Gardens, the fern-slick hills
of Dublin, outpacing the harehounds and curricles—
one Sunday in Brighton, outpacing a froth
of four-horse coaches. Past shepherds,
chemists, past Schubert perhaps, or Wordsworth,
the flutter-pulse of wheel-rims and tailcoats
a counterpoint, a phantom delight. One year,

two. Another. Then, in the up-gust nudges
of treadles and pedal cranks, they were lifted—

warm saddles, wheels sissing—to the lofts
and attics of a dozen countries, packed
in with the tinwear. And for a handful of decades

taken down. Half in mockery, in some land-locked
flicker for flight, grandcousins, neighbors
pushed off into glides, became for the sudden
faces in windowframes, for strollers
just passing the pollard willows, a bevy
of pelicans—or in the certain clipped
half-lights of winter, storm petrels,

death swans in their peach-legged strokings.
For the walkers of Austria, France, for the housebound,
the children, they were omens, sorcerers,
counterpoint. For the child van Gogh, perhaps,
looking up from his magpie's nest—there,
backlit on the heath ridge, leg pumps
and spokes indistinguishable—they were
the coil-spun circuits of stars, drawn
down through the bracken by folly, by rage,
and all the human urgencies.

THE APISCULPTURES

And today she has circled the orchard.
Step, then step, the steel ball of the femur-head
slip-slipping through its Teflon socket.
Just a smoothness now, where a rasp
had been, an arthritic package
gouged to the grate of a ratchet wheel. And sunlight,

on the mint, the knobbed joints of peach trees.
It is noon. She passes a run
of bee boxes, tarpapered, on stilts,
like the marsh-front cabins of coastal towns,
then stops at a weathered closet—a studio
of sorts, for the drape-cast hive-works of bees.

Apisculptures. One colony, one common shape—
rake or shoe-tree, a wax-buffed wagon wheel—
and, shut in the closet for days, the bees
will take or reject it, will wait
in a thick belt at the doorframe

or begin their rhythmic spinning.
A plane covered. A spoke. Cell by hexagonal cell,
a building—outward, upon—one sloping lobe, another,
now and then, a disk, a circle of comb
suspended in the darkness like a supper plate.

In the corners of her house the finest linger,
preened with a water-pick. And oddly,

.

she thinks, turning now, stepping off
toward the fenceline, left leg lumbering, the right
exhausted, just a feather touch, it is
the human shape they favor, time after time,
shoe-tree, helmet, the curved tines
of a dressmaker's armature. Gold lobes,

then a cross-stitch of frame below—arresting,
irresistible—like the acid-cast films of her body
clamped to a viewing screen.
Where the femur reached up to the socket,
a beakerwork. A product. A globe
of synthetic filaments, molecule on molecule, as if

the vapor-snaps and S-tubes of science were saying
Let us start with the made and blossom.
With the made, then the petals of flesh
in their mauve expansions. Or the bees

just there in their warm closet,
thick with its thrum notes, its suggestions
of shoulder, waist, the fan of a cupped hand,
Let us start with the blossom. . . .

AUDUBON'S BORDER BOY

He is sketching.
First the vein and stamen twitch-strokes
of the white hydrangea, thumb cocked,
three fingers crooked inward—like the cramp
an ice ball offers to the freezing hand.
Then the push, pull, push, pull of
leaves filling in. A stalk. Two joints
where the lemon-necked birds might fasten.

At his back, a stretch of magnolia trees
drops, then is sheared
by the influx lappings of the Mississippi.
Last autumn, he watched from a cargo arc
as his family on the shoreline was reduced
in increments, like the buff, thick candlesticks

that cast to the cabin walls
the neck curls and shadowed chinline of Audubon.
They have traveled eight months—all the widgeons
and hooded mergansers dissected to wands, an acorn
of craw. And for him, the black backdrop canopy
of forest dissected as well, drawn out to
the elements. He is thirteen. Perhaps he will travel

westward, through the bracken and cane-vines, to a separate,
uncatalogued vegetation. A family
from Fort Mandan, he was told, hungry
on the wide plains, once roasted the bulbs of tulips
to a blue mash—and the daffodils they had carried,

the thick narcissus—then entered
their wagons as bulb-sized hailstones
pocked and toppled the carriage mules.

There is an urgency in the thrush, he has learned,
in the partridge and warbler, to enter the backdrop canopy
like a black sky. An absorption there, for an instant,
then a singling out, like eyes
adjusting to candlelight. And perhaps that family

joined them, looking down from their wagons
to the stunned faces of the lost mules,
as the source of their violation
slipped away in increments. Ears, jawline,
and below, the vast, white absorption of the plains.
A blindness perhaps, then. Then the singling out:
half hail, half the spiked white grasses without names.

BIRD IN SPACE: FIRST STUDY

Constantin Brancusi

Nothing grows in the shadow of great trees...
And yet, in a wine cask's shadowy tube—oak aged
and curved to a first-growth trunk—
his legs inched up from his ankles.
He was sixteen, alone. By a storefront window
in Craiova, great breaths of chocolate
sighing out from a churn stick

held him. And the pattern of wheat dust
on silos, the pattern of corn
on a pulpy cob, like the grid marks in squid.
Hunger. Its spidery grip. And then he was hired,
dipped by the wrists into wine casks.
Small, slender—the restaurant above him
no more than a wind of garlic—he lathered, scrubbed,

all the pips slipping out from the rough-hewn wood,
all the bristle tips, esters,
and the odors of yeast, wet wool, the wine sludge
curved to the shape of his knees, his fingertips
curved to the oak blebs: body and barrel
in equal exchange—a melding, a kiss.

Days passed. A year. Often at dusk
he read cards at the restaurant tables, watched
the wide Rumanian faces swell, withdraw.
From a circle of Chariots, of Towers
and delicate Hanged Men, a fear would begin,

brushing up through each face like a wine flush.
Enigmas. The queer burbles of candle wax.
Then a cello spun out its long notes, binding,
cupping them all to the known earth,

as, morning by morning, the slats of an oak wine cask
cupped his small body. Sometimes
he sang there—cello songs, drawn down to the tempo
of bristle tips, splinters. Sometimes he studied
his hoop-slice of sky: looped from the ceiling, from
strings like the rays of geometry, amber onions,
three halved by the barrel rim's sharp circumference,
beets and beet tufts, and, weekly,

the marbled hind legs of a roebuck.
Globe shapes, light-polished, or cragged
by a smatter of earth. Then weekly,
arcing into his view from a fuller body,
two thighs, two hocks, pulled tight at the hooves
by a thread of rawhide: pale form in a fixed arc,
like the memory of motion, like a bird stalled
in the ice-winds of space, its stillness, flight.

THE GRANDSIRE BELLS

At first quick glance and lingering second,
the five, sludge-smeared miners on the roadway—
through this pre-morning light, with their shock
of canary in its braided cage—
might have seemed to the five ringers approaching

like a portrait of memory, like the sway
and blear of themselves in memory: the bend
of bootsoles in the myrtle grass, black
caps, yellow lantern flame, the knapsack stings
of rhubarb and mildew. And the village

below, coal fires granting to the fresh day
plumes in the fashion of cypresses—base knot,
stalk, the splintering crown-tip—a kind
of memory also, as the ringers trudged
up the hillside, past the miners and smoke strings,

past the fluted iron churchyard fence, the dollops
of marble headstones. Then into the breezeway,
where belfry steps accepted the trudge,
and the bells, above, waited. Five. In a blend
of copper and tin, each shouldered the hub ring

of a great wheel, the bell ropes lashed to spokes
and threaded, the soft-tufted cordage
dangling down to the ringers like a spray
of air roots. With the motion of climbing
the treble was cocked, pulled up to suspend

.

at the balance point, waist and mouth-edge
inverted, hovering. Then the others cocked,
turned up, each ton of fish scale–glistening
arc at rest on a pin-tip of stay.
And toppled. One after one, treble, second,

third, fourth, tenor, toppled. Quick pump and spillage,
like heartbeats. Again, the ringers releasing
the strike and hum notes, handstroke to backstroke,
the bells pulled up, up, the snapping ropes wound
up, tail tufts and sally-grips in the jig-play

of dancers. All morning, the swinging
treble wound through its hunt path, a nudge
into second ring, third, fourth, and the second
replacing the tenor bell, and the third knocked
into lead. In the village the day

was a braiding of change-rings, notes swelling,
fading, as the bells turned. In the bracken
and mine shafts. In the foundry, when the forge
bellows hushed and the furnace tapway
spilled a rush of smoking bronze down brick-

lined troughs in the earth floor. Bell notes. When
bronze curled down through buried bell molds, cut half-rings
in the earth, cut bell shapes. When the cupped clay
flared and stiffened. Bell notes. Change upon change.
Then ending. Ending. In an instant, closing back

.

in their first order. All ringers for that second
claiming past, present, like walkers on a roadway:
in the half-light of morning, one shock
of canary in a braided cage,
one curve of lantern flame approaching.

ABOUT THE AUTHOR

Linda Bierds's poetry has appeared in *The New England Review and Breadloaf Quarterly*, *The New Yorker*, *The Atlantic*, *The Massachusetts Review*, *Poetry Northwest*, *The Seattle Review*, *Field*, and *The Hudson Review*. Her first collection was *Flights of the Harvest-Mare*, published in 1985. Her second, *The Stillness, the Dancing*, was published by Henry Holt in 1988.

The recent recipient of an Ingram Merrill Foundation Award, Bierds also has been awarded a National Endowment for the Arts Fellowship in Poetry, an Artist Trust Foundation of Washington Fellowship in Poetry, and a Pushcart Prize in Poetry. She lives in Seattle, Washington.